Welcome

Introduction

I hope you enjoy the poetry and illustrations.
Most of the poems came straight from my heart.
I started out with a few illustrations and then decided
to do more. Some came from inside me and just flowed out,
Including the front and back covers, others were inspired by
other artists works. The peacock lovebirds were inspired by a wonderful
artist's work I found on the internet and the ocean wave painting by the
photographer who goes inside waves to take his pictures.

It was a lot of fun making the illustrations and I never would have made them if it were not for me putting the book together, so I hope this may inspire anyone who wants to move forward with a goal to start and be positive as you never know what doors it will open for you and how you will enjoy fulfilling your new aspirations and goals. I hope above all things whatever you may do that you pray and allow God through his Son to guide you. All things may not bring us happiness now under the present conditions on earth, but He promises a better future for us soon.

I feel most people have deep feelings about things that they have never put into words and hope they find the poems enjoyable. If you have never felt many of the things I wrote about regarding love, or if your love has not endured, the most important love of all is with God Himself/YAHAWAY/Jehovah and His Son Jesus Christ/YAHASHUA, although their names may be known to you slightly differently.

Rita MacDonald, thank you for your motherly love that inspired poems, 'Beautiful Lady' and 'Soft Sweet Flowers of Love'. I also thank my own loving mother. My faith poem expresses the Faith I am always striving to have and keep. I wish I could say I always have had this perfect faith, but I wrote this after having lacked so much of it. I know the only hope for any of us is to have faith in God and Jesus Christ His Son, and so we have to put our full trust in them for our lives now and the future. I thank them for their help and inspiration with this book, that I hope you will enjoy reading.

Table of Contents

Order this book online at www.trafford.com
or email orders@trafford.com

Most Trafford titles are also available at major online book retailers.

Print information available on the last page.

ISBN: 978-1-4251-1320-9 (sc)

Trafford rev. 4/7/2015

 www.trafford.com
North America & international
toll-free: 1 888 232 4444 (USA & Canada)
fax: 812 355 4082

Faith

Faith can move a mountain
And guide you on your way
Though doors may shut around you
open your Heart and Pray
Put Faith in Him who can save you
Reach out to Him today
Let Him move the mountains
And let Him light your way
A God of Love can lead you
through the darkness of the night
if you reach out with all your heart
He'll be your strength and might
He'll fight your battles for you
If you trust with all your soul
Make Him the light of your life
So He can make you whole
His Son gave His precious life
in obedience to Him
And through their love can save us
From our many sins
Trust in His LOVE and KINDNESS
And in His POWER too
So with faith in your heart
move forward
He'll show His love for you

He could never be unfaithful
It's impossible for Him
So trust in Him with all your heart and
Let Him answer you
With His Love He'll help you
May your heart's desires come true

Portrait of A Man

Your lips are ripe peaches..luscious and full, soft and tender
red as roses

Your eyes are like a lake that reflect in the sky above....
Rich and Alive with Life
beautiful and enchanting......where doves kiss

Where soft gentle breezes sway hanging branches...
where the sun sparkles and the moon glows
And a richness of life around and within
to reflect your Love, your Heart, your Soul, your Mind
Your face is like a colorful flower that glows with brightness
Your hair is a crown of silk that grows up like a field of wild grass
and caresses your head like soft feathers

Your body is strong like a young warrior that reflects the masculine
strength of God and the blessings He gave us in beauty
Your chest is like a breastplate of armor, yet soft and warm and sensual looking
Protective and comforting

You're a man

Your arms hold love and tenderness and strength in them
Your hips are like a young bull's...strong and powerful,
your legs are a masculine work of art.
Your searching feet have carried you through some city streets....
Your Real beauty is within your heart and mind where lies the real person who is what
you really are   One whom I hope will continue to grow in love with God and
become His true Son...Fully reflecting His Strength, Beauty, Righteousness, Truth,

Manliness, Gentleness, Kindness, Faithfulness,

                Love and **Godliness** forever

A JEWEL

You're a shining jewel...like a star in the sky...
You're gentle and kind
and so funny I think I'll love you forever
I wish you were mine...Right now
I wish you happiness forever
Your voice and laughter...are a bird's song
singing a melody...of life...and love
with music that gently reaches my ears and fills my heart and mind and soul
Your words are scholarly
from a deep intellect—like an uncut stone that shines with brilliance
Reach for the sun and grow straight for it
but bend with the wind, gain strength and be strong
Your heart is as sweet as a flower that gives its soft scent
but strong like a lion's...you will fight for what you really want
You're as open as a child
but Knowing and deep—as the man whom you really are
I love you
I wish you happiness forever under the loving care of our Father in Heaven
and His Son our Savior, who also loves us

A MAN

I love a man who I wish was mine
truer eyes I've never seen
His face and eyes show his heart and his
whole soul
even when he's mean...he's beautiful,
because I see the man within
he has the heart of a man...and a child.

The Orator Man

Your nose speaks to me of your elegance, power and
determination to move forward in victory with masculine
strength and dignity. Your light green eyes are like jewels
that sparkle with light. Your lips are like a bed of rose petals
inviting me to lie down and be caressed by your tender
gentle kisses. Your chest is warm, loving and strong. Your
embracing arms hold power and comfort. Your legs are like
a gazelle's, lean and strong. The key to your heart comes
from Above and the combination is in your hands to
give to the one whom you choose share in your love.

GIFTS FROM ABOVE

I always knew there was a jewel out there somewhere,
but when I least expected it
God sent me a treasure chest
More beautiful than I ever could have imagined
Where beautiful different colored lights beamed out and
reflected the light above,
so that I just had to look within,
And when I looked inside
I saw all beautiful different gems
filled with color that sparkled on every side
with all brilliant beautiful colors of light
and as I pick them up in my hands they sparkle all over
and reflect all the beautiful gifts of your being
and your personality, all the different gifts that you have
that give beauty and glow on every side

Every way I look I see more beauty radiating and glowing out from within
As I look, the lights beam out all around me and as I hold them up they sparkle and glow through my
fingers and into my eyes. Every trait is a gift from above that shows
God's Wisdom, Beauty and Love.
You have so many gifts - Your light has entered my mind, my heart, my soul and touched my spirit
within - my very being and become Part of me. They reflect all through me and light up my soul with joy
and happiness and beauty that I see and feel glowing all through my soul and heart and mind..
Sometimes I feel I am just growing inside and my heart is alive and moving with beauty that
glows from you, And my warm hands bring warmth to the stones as we share something together. They
seem to take on an extra brilliance as they come closer to my heart and eyes and we then reflect each
other with our gifts from God Above and glow together, becoming part of one another in Love.
Hopefully with God's and His Son's blessings, it will be forever. Thank you my God and my Savior for
sending me this very special treasure. Please help us to gently care for one another under your radiating
Love that shines down on us like sunbeams and enters our hearts, our minds, our souls - Your life giving
Spirit. Please help us to honor you and bring Glory to your NAME forever because of your
GOODNESS and BEAUTY and LOVE .

P.S. I did see a lump of coal at the bottom, but I think it's turning into a diamond.

ALIVE AS ONE

I want you to live inside me
inside my heart, my mind, my spirit, my body,
I want you to LIVE inside of me and be Part of me
I want us to be part of each other
I know with God's blessings we would be happy
and have great joy with each other
Part of what moves each of us
I want you to be part of what I feel
Part of what I give, part of what I live...forever
I want you to be in me always,
to live to grow, to share to know
the love of GOD, the love of each other

Happy to live, happy to share to grow and multiply, to become one
To live as one in heart and mind and spirit and body and yet be separate
Like pillars supporting the same building, like stars that make the sky softly glow and give
light to each other that is felt and reflected and even others can see. Two that become one in
being like two dancers intertwined whose eyes gaze deeply and move to the same music as One
with Energy, Passion, Tenderness, Sensuality, Sensitively feeling each others movements,
feelings and desires in every way
Separate and One at the same time

DO YOU FEEL WHAT I FEEL

Do you feel the way that I feel when you're near me and I see your eyes? Does your Body come alive....
Does your heart beat faster....Do you breathe harder....and deeper do you love life more
Do you feel joy...and love and peace and goodness Do feelings surge through you that you've never felt
before Do you want your Lips to be on Mine...do you want my eyes to stare into yours Do you want to
feel me next to you, inside you and move your heart...like you move mine... Do you want us to grow
together so that we really are one Does your heart wrench with pain... Do you feel what I feel when I
think you don't care In the depths of despair...does your heart wrench with pain... Do you feel the
loneliness I feel...when I don't have you here...Do you miss me like I miss you? In the depth of my soul I
feel such pain without you...life seems so lost - seems so low

I want you to know I love you so much,
I just don't know what to do but rely on God. I miss you...I care
I love you so much
Does your heart soar and feel like it's flying in the sky...like mine does when I hear your voice
Does your heart jump for joy when you come here anytime of day and hear my voice,
like mine does when you're outside and I hear yours?
Am I too sick to be with you right now? I hope GOD heals me
Am I too sick to love
No, that would be impossible
Because my heart is alive with love from my FATHER in HEAVEN and HIS BEAUTIFUL SON
I only hope one day soon I will get the opportunity to show you what I truly have been blessed to feel for
you and with GOD'S blessing—that you feel the same.
I love you from the top of your head to the tips of your toes,
from your heart to your soul, from your inside to your outside.
Do I bring you joy like you bring me
Do you know how much I feel?
Will you love me forever, as I love you?

WHAT IS LOVE
What is Love? After all I try to figure out why I fell so deeply
What does it do to you
it takes your mind, your heart and moves you
Do I really have my senses, do I really know what I'm doing?
Why am I pulled so powerfully,
Why do I want to be with you so much
be near you so close
and be part of you so deeply, so joyously
What happened to me?
Yet, yes I know you are beautiful
yes, I know you have many gifts
There are numerous beautiful people with gifts, but you came and let you light shine into me
You let me feel your tender feelings and I cared for you
You let me see how sensitive you are and I feel for you
I saw your pain and I cried
I saw your joy and I was lifted up
I saw your love and I loved you

You let me see your strength and I look to you and want to share with you and support you
You let me see your beauty
let me see all your emotions and make me feel for you and love you
when you're kind, when you're not kind
when you're nice, when you're loving
I love all of you and want to grow with you toward our God and His Son
You and your light became part of me, became part of my cells
became part of my body, my mind, my heart, my spirit, My Love
Part of what moves me inside   Now, can I rip my finger off? No, I can't do that
Can I rip my heart out? No, I can't do that
Can I rip you out of my cells, my body, my mind, my heart, my soul? No, I can't do that!
I want you and I want no one but you
because I truly love you for who you are
I don't want another man to come near me
I don't want his lips to touch mine
I want only your lips on mine
I want only your body next to me
I want only to feel the warmth of your chest next to mine
I want only your face next to mine, only your breath on my face
only your emotions and your voice near me
I've heard that it takes seven years for your body to make all new cells
How can I tare you out of me? I can't do it, I don't want to do it, because you gave me something
beautiful and new in my life, you gave me a joy that lifts my spirit and makes me feel like I'm flying,
you gave me a joy that goes through my whole body and lifts me high and enlivens my body, my mind,
my spirit, my heart.
I care about your feelings , your life, your happiness. I truly love you and hope God and His Son
bless me to be part of what makes you happy, what brings you joy
I want to share with you—
joy and peace and happiness and fulfillment, passion, intimacy, love, tenderness, growth,
Spirituality, love of our God and His Son
When I put a little seed into the ground and it sprouts, it absorbs all the nutrients from the ground,
the minerals and all the good the ground has to give
and so they have become part of each other
and when you put your beauty into me you truly became part of me
and now it's with you—my heart, my soul and my body want to live,
to grow together
and to become One.

LOVE CAN BE STRANGE

Love is sometimes strange
Where is the man I once loved?
He seems almost like a stranger
Love doesn't die by itself
Love lives forever but doesn't always burn hot
Love can cool down when breath isn't breathed into it
Love can die to an ember when is isn't fed and nurtured
The passion can die if it isn't fed
Love can die if it is crushed
But you can love the memory forever of what you once shared
Or you can hide it deep and cover it over and just be friends
Love can be cooled down and put out if it is watered and not fed
Love where are you
It almost looks like you're dead
Yet, yes I know that God and His Son can resurrect the dead -
Can bring life back to the lifeless
So I am happy to leave all things in His loving wonderful hands and
trust in Him and His Son
Thank you my God for leading me in all things
May your will be done please,
in your magnificent mercy

Peace

I finally have peace
I want you to know....It's all in God's hands
I trust Him so
I really do love you....And God and His Son
May His will be done.

This Thing Called Love

My love flew High in the sky

like a Bird Soaring High in the air

Then it came

down

and ate a worm!

My love flew high in the sky

floating in the air like a bird

with a clear view on a bright sunny day,

below the white fluffy clouds

and then it came

down to earth!

But free again to fly

and soar High in the Sky

This thing called Love

Inside My Heart

How did you reach inside me so deeply
how did you find that place in my heart
how did you do it ever so sweetly
what was it that you did so delicately and completely?
You let me see you....you let me see you
and taste you and touch you and feel you
in my heart
Now, like a tree with its sap flowing up
You're flowing in me to all my parts.

Why

Why did you reach inside my soul
Why did you take my heart in your hands
And want to make us whole
Why did you draw me to you
Why did you reach so deep inside of me

And stir my heart to yearn for you
To burn for you
With a passion that I feel in my heart
That I feel in my soul
It burns through me
like a smoldering flame
When will you hold me
When will I feel you   When will you
satisfy this fire in my soul, In my heart
When will we be whole
I feel we are already one
somewhere deep inside...I know that
connection is there, but when oh when
will we really be whole
I want only you
No one else can do
My love it too real
My Love is too true

18

Do You Know

You took a spade and opened the ground
and put my love inside and put some dirt on top
Will this love Grow
Will it Sprout
Will it die like a grave
I want to reach out
God's will be done through His Son

FEEL LOVE GROW

When you give LOVE
give it freely
because it's the most beautiful gift that you can give
When you give love you are Your Most Beautiful
you Light up with an *Energy*
You become beautiful and beauty FLOWS from you and grows inside of you
that you can feel and others can see
It is a gift from God
Just what is it you want to grow in you and fill you up...Love and beauty or ugliness?
When you plant, water and nurture a garden, it takes work
to do this feels satisfying, sometimes it's Hard work
sometimes it's Refreshing
and when you see the fruits of your labor, you feel satisfied
When someone is ugly with you and mean,
if you treat them the same way, you've allowed their ugliness to take root in you and you've become like them and
you actually REFLECT the same ugliness and anger,
but when you don't reflect them, then you have not become like them.
If you join in their dance, then you've become *their* partner
and your feet move together in the same steps as you unwittingly hold hands and your energies and beings swirl together
as if in a spiders web or a wrestler's ring
Humbly ask God to help you create your own beautiful dance and walk and follow God and His Son and then the person
may want to join you and you have kept true to what is good, whether they join you in love or not and you will
feel beautiful, happy, blessed and peaceful and you will feel true growth
This is easier said than done -   When you're in trouble, pray right away. Pray every day and ask God to guide you and to
please Him and His Son ... And don't allow anything to make you falter in your steps and in following God and His Son.
When you let only love grow in you, it *radiates* outward
and they feel your love and it enters them instead of pain and
your love sinks into them

And helps love to grow and restore and heal them, If they don't want to change at least they haven't changed you
and they may feel ashamed and want to join you and love can grow in them and reflect the love you gave them
and in return you will receive love instead of more ugliness and you will feel beauty inside of you and a peace and a calm
and it is a gift from God, because all love comes from God
When you see a little bird that's hurt and he needs your help and you pick him up and you see how beautiful he is,
If he hadn't come so close you may have never known his delicate true beauty in detail
And so you received a blessing and you feel good, because you did good.
When you see your fellow man in pain don't turn your back
Isn't he/she worth more than a little bird?
When you see someone in need reach out and help them
And you always get a blessing in return
When a lost animal comes to your door who is hungry and weak, won't you feed him and give him shelter
or take him to a shelter, hoping someone can help him and give him love?
You may not be able to feed every lost animal in the world, but when one comes to your door, won't you feed it
and help others who need help when you can?
When you see a lost soul won't you help him as much as an animal?
Won't you help them to grow? If you see them in need won't you help them?
Ask yourself, did God's Son die for them? Won't you give them love freely?
God says this is what we should do
You will feel love inside you that even *others* see
and You will *feel* and see more beauty

You will be more beautiful.

A Waking Flower

Like a **flower** in morning that is kissed by the dew
whose petals open gently to greet the morning light
so I awake to you Father, every day
May Your Holy Spirit flow down like a splash of light from
the sun with power and warming rays of energy that
come from You
You help us to feel refreshed and strengthened
as we awake to a new day

May we grow toward you as a flower toward the sun
Your life and Your light give us strength
May Your Spirit flow through us and enliven our hearts,
our minds, our bodies, to serve you and to know you
tenderly. - You and Your Son and to feel Your Spirit
Energizing us and directing our lives so that we may
through Your Son and Your Spirit serve You as One.

Earth's Waters

D. Cerelli

Oh what have they done to one so sweet
You were fresh and clear and bright
You sparkled like diamonds do in light
And danced with moonbeams in the night
Now you flow with my tears for all the years
You've been corrupted, ruined and hurt
Where is the life you once held when you were young and fancy free
I'm afraid there really isn't much of it left for me to see
Come back sweet waters and fill the earth
Give joy to them as you once so sweetly gave to me

L. Doyle

Our Glorious Home Restored

A soft silvery moon with twinkling starlights on a blanket of soft black velvet gives me a restful sleep. You rise up in the morning with golden warm rays to help me gently arise, as the little birds sing me songs and you awaken the flowers. Life starts to bustle in the hills and in the cities. Your blue-green waves capped with white foam kiss our sandy shores. From your rich green hills I look out upon your vast blue-green oceans as I sit beneath your fragrant flowering trees and eat of your juicy fruit. The birds and bees fly and float on wings of joy. Fish happily swim in the brooks as the animals interact in their life's struggles...they have their joy and pain. From the tops of the white snow-covered mountains to the blue swaying sea and green lush forests to the sandy deserts and fields of golden wheat, I enjoy the life and the glorious beauty you share with me. Each day is greeted with a new entrance and exit, with curtains of purple, orange, pink and lavender on your blue skies. Yet, like tears from the Heavens, raindrops fall as we face our joys and pain and wars, sickness and dying. We're given a golden hope that all will be restored and only Love, Good Health and Eternal Life will Remain. Rev 21: 1-5, M't 5:5, Psl *37:9-29, (Catholic Bible Psl *36); Prov 2:21,22;

I Wish I Knew Then

An old man with wisdom slowly walked by and said; "I wish I knew then what I know now"
The young woman heard him and wanted to know too
So she could learn from him and not walk in his shoes
So, he turned to her with care in his eyes, but he said only; "You'll find out", You'll find out"
She just couldn't figure out why he wouldn't share, so he could help her life be free from failure and care
for she knew not of what he meant and couldn't understand his strange chant
but wanted desperately to learn her share
Twenty years went by and she remembered the old man
and at last she understood of what he meant
and how much wisdom there was in what he had said
for the knowledge was finally in her grasp
she learned her lessons well
for the lessons were already spent
And Finally, finally she knew what he meant...

Life After the Fall

A young tender twig grows toward the sun
it grows mighty and tall, it becomes a magnificent tree
filled with lush green leaves that bring beauty to all who
gaze at its splendor. Lovers sit under its boughs and breathe
in the fresh air. It gives a living breath to all...then its leaves
change and bring a brilliant display of color with reds,
oranges and yellows to fascinate us all
But at the height of its beauty the beautiful leaves start to
wrinkle and shrivel and fall, cascading in the wind with one last curtain call and before long
they're all gone. Only a bare barren tree remains, but all is not lost after all. The leaves go
back to the ground and silently give life back, so the tree regains its strength in its seeming sleep
to come to life again, blooming and giving beauty to all. Those resting in the ground will again
grow straight and tall. It is promised that they will rise and bloom again when things are
better and life and beauty are without end.

Beautiful Lady

Although we may be miles apart
The love you gave is still in my heart
Wherever you go, whatever you do
This love will always remain for you
So never think that you're forgotten
You know that can't be true
A love that sweet will always be
Here in my heart for you

Grandpop

Grandpop, how I long to see your face again
sending me love like you did before
when I was a babe on the living room floor
Such a lovely way you had of expressing yourself
Such kindness you sent floating through the air and into my heart
and made me smile right from my start
Thank you for giving all you could give, though you left me so soon
and I had to live - without you, but you stayed in my heart and in
my Mind through all this time...Your love stayed deep in my soul
and one day I hope to see you again when we are made whole
I hope I will give you joy as you gave me and
Love You Forever in Eternity

Kiss Me Under The Stars

Kiss me under the stars tonight   Dance with me in the soft moonlight
Lay your body next to mine   And sleep with me as our souls entwine
Let the stars be our only canopy
and the sounds of the leaves rustling in the cool night breeze
be our midnight melody, while our soft-spoken voices whisper our song
When the morning comes with the kiss of the dew
Our love will surely shine through   As little birds sweet songs in the
bushes nearby gently wake us   And the sun rises up to greet our day
May our morning kiss bring us an intoxicating high   As soft scents
of flowers drift our way   And sweet smells of roses and lilacs soften
our day   May our love go with us all day long like a locket in our
hearts to sing us a song   And with God's blessings give us
strength and peace to carry on

27

Soft Sweet Flowers of Love

Dear

Her words flow like sweet Flowers
from Lips of Honey
That Float through the Air
with a Fragrant Scent
and Lift your Spirit
so that Life Seems Sweeter ↓

They Blossom in Your Heart and Mind
and Bring Joy to Your Spirit

Such a Wonderful Gift from GOD
Flows Freely from the Beautiful Lady's Heart
as she shares with others

Her Joy Humility and Love ↓

With Love,

Life

Can the eye say I am better than the toe
Or can the leg say I am better than the nose
They all belong to one and are One
Can the piano say I am better than the axe
for without the axe there would be no piano
They were made by man as instruments of man to be used by him
They didn't create themselves
So, as with man...All Men are one and created by One
Can one man say he is better than another

We are All instruments through which
Love and other gifts can flow
and harmonize like the best orchestra
Man didn't make himself, so how can he brag or feel haughty
Praise goes to God the Creator
One man will brag and say he is better because of his gifts and yet someone else bragged because they had those same gifts - His parents did not possess
Let life and Love Flow through you, not Swelling you so you would Break with pressure, but so you can freely Receive and Give

 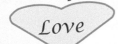

Love

You come to me for love
My love is like a sweet clear brook
Full of Life
Bursting, bubbling splashing, Inviting you to be...
Refreshed and to drink
To make what is me...in you
Living and part of your being
To take with you wherever you are
And to return again
To be separate and one at the same time
I give you my life and you are one with me
My waters are cool and Living
Like a well they are always there for you
to draw from

If my Love were shallow my waters could dry up, but on deep examination I see they are connected to the deepest water flowing in the earth, to life itself, that will forever be...always being replenished from a living deep force   To see you I could shoot forth and surround and capture you but I would be killing you, drowning your love and life   You draw from me what you can and in being separate
We become ONE

Love's Ingredients

First say a prayer, then start with pure water

very gently add the ingredients

Carefully place them in one by one at just the right time
Not too early, not too late

Make sure it's based on a rich hardy substance

Place in your meat   Add your potatoes

Add your onions and your vegetables

Sprinkle in your measure of Spices to wake things up
and add some zing

And gently stir them in
Let them all Simmer together Slowly

Don't turn your flame too high or it'll cook too fast and
Burn Everything Up

Don't cook it too slow or it'll go bad

Keep that fire burning
Not too hot not too low

Let it simmer, cook gently and slowly

'Watch It Carefully'

And with your own loving hands stir

And when it is done

what will we have

Satisfaction in "OUR LOVE"

War-My Brother

My mother gave birth to a child, who moved away
from here
I didn't see that child, for many, many a year

Then one day his country came to fight with mine
And I saw this child in battle...among those first in line

How could I hurt her son, he was a brother of mine
I saw his beautiful face...
looking much like my own child, Elase

His eyes met mine and we cried
as we shook in our tender embrace
How good it felt to hold - this child with the loving face

I could no longer fight.....and kill for the kings at war
I decided that my love for my brother
was a part of what I'm living here for

In this system
the battle will always rage for one reason or another

but, whatever those reasons are
I cannot kill my brother

You may label me a coward or a traitor, but I tell you
It takes courage to stand up for your beliefs
if you disagree with your neighbor

MY BEAUTIFUL COUNTRY HOME

My beautiful country home is filled with sweet flowers and beautiful green trees where birds sing a gentle melody.   I have rolling green hills where the children can play and ride on our horses. As I look to the tops of the mountains and see the blue skies above, with white puffy clouds floating by, I know they were made with such tender care and love. My Father gave me a country mansion, it's so beautiful with its windows to the stars. I can see the blue heavens with streaks of lavender, pink and sunshine-orange in the sky and clouds and in the evening when the sun goes down I see twinkling stars above that light my way and help me to feel alive and not alone. What a beautiful mansion I have. I grow fruit trees to satisfy my desires and the fragrant perfumed sweet scents flow through the air and into my body and become part of me. I have little creatures that enjoy life here and all kinds of animals; horses, cows and others and birds with colors that they flutter through the air...red, blue, yellow, orange, pink, and more. They sing me light delicate little songs to lift my spirit and give me joy as they fly and sit in my trees. I have friends here to love and share my life, along with my animal companions. I soak in the radiating sun as the mighty oceans gently roll in. Sometimes I swim or walk along and as I dip my feet, the ocean sprays me with light droplets of water that refreshes my soul while the clean salt-air brings a fresh scent. The huge aquarium I own has porpoises and dolphins and many life forms.   It's an unearned gift from my Father. I breathe in the clean fresh air from all the living things that He gave me. My home is alive and it breathes with me, when I breathe out it breathes in and it purifies my air. It shares my life.   As I stand on the mountains He gave me I can feel His energy flow through me and I realize His Spirit enters me and makes me feel light, like I can fly through the air and I realize I'm part of the universe as we all move around together on our Home. My home is so beautiful, we have everything we need to be happy, we have fruit trees, lush vegetation, sparkling brooks, mountains, oceans... **Love** and **peace**. How happy I am to be blessed with my beautiful country home-'**The Earth', in God's promised new Paradise.**

Children

Truly, children are like arrows
With the force of Love
Parents help them Fly away
If the wind blows and a storm comes
even like a young Bird who tries his
tender wings
Let them fly so they can reach their
goals
and gain strength along the way
Inside of them they must decide which
way to go
God has given us All gifts
the parents must not believe they
know better what the child should do
with his skills
If given a packet of mixed seeds that
you water with love
You let them grow to be what they are
You wouldn't pluck an orchid looking
for lemons
Give them all the love you can give
Raise them in the Light of God's Love
and ask **Him** to guide their way as
they Grow and fly away

Fly away, Fly away, Fly away free

May the Love we've shared

Bring your Heart back to me

Let Your Heart Sing

What song will you sing today
Will it be loud will it be strong
Will it be a song of love...
Love for who you are and what you do
Will you give me a clean street on which to drive safely
Will you pack my groceries with a smile and help make my day pleasant
Will you keep my house clean by taking away my trash
Will you paint my house a pretty color so I can enjoy it more
Whatever you do let your heart sing
Let it sing a happy song so you can work with pride
And be glad of your efforts
Let your heart sing and find what satisfies you
Bring out your melody, God gave it to you so you can find your dream
Reach out today to do what you love
Whatever you do, do it with joy, kindness and Love
Love for your God above and His Son and love for All He has blessed you with
Listen to the guidance of His Spirit on the strings of your heart and trust in Him
Put God first and He will guide you on your path

Earth's Perfect Hope

Our Beautiful planet, **blue**, green and many colors of the **Rainbow**
Has been stained **Red** from **blood**, killing and sin
Its glaciers are melting away
Polar bears and others surviving on the ice are becoming fearful, suffering and dying
Their home is melting into the sea
Its heated waters are raging forth like a bubbling cauldron,
while fierce monstrous tempests march on and attack from the sky
The earth is shaking, spewing out and exploding as with hot angry outbursts
Like a **bleeding heart** that cries as teardrops fall our **skies** bring forth rain
as the oceans rise and rage forth like
an earth whose **heart** is overflowing with pain
Our life-giving planet is melting and burning in agony
The colorful coral reefs instead of giving life are dying, turning poisonous as life seeps out of their blanched white bleak skeletons
The leaves in the rain forest are burning away and so the sun sears the skins of the animals
They are forced to abandon their homes
They must move away from the equator to escape their old friend
Our life-giving sun with its warm rays is now like an **angry warrior**, searing through and
Burning us for all our careless greed and the things that we've done
Man, the animals, the fish and insects are dying
The honeybees are disappearing by the millions
Is this due to man's hand?
Without pollination life would cease in our land
Children are taken as slaves and they see death and sorrow without hope of tomorrow

The most intelligent creation living on the face of the earth, the glorious pinnacle and the supposed caretaker cannot save us
Man's handiwork is bringing our earth and all its life to the brink of extinction
But God says He will save us
He says that, there will be a great disaster but that as in Noah's Day, there will be survivors
He promises that through His Kingdom Government that we pray for to 'Come' M't 6:10
And let His will on earth be done, and ruled fully by His Son Psl 2; Prov 21:1,2,....
The earth and the meek who do His will shall be saved. Matt 5:5
Then soon the day will come when all the earth shall sing in glory to the True Ruler in Heaven
Then the survivors and the resurrected of mankind will never again experience a global disaster.
All the animals will be peaceable and the lion will eat straw
and lie down with the lamb. Isa 11:6-9
The flowers will sing a glorious tune of sweet fragrance and beauty. The **mountains** will shout high with majestic power and radiance and the deserts will **blossom forth as a rose**
The people will sing a beautiful song of Joy, Thankfulness and **Love** to their God forever
The earth will be filled to the tops of the mountains with food, happiness and life without end Isa 35:1-10
So, while things look bleak, yes do what you can, don't give up hope, but don't put your trust in man
Put your trust and your faith in God, for true salvation for All the Earth Rev/Apoc 1:1; 21:1-5; 20:4-6; 5:9,10; 14:1-5

Is In His Hands

Printed in the United States
by Baker & Taylor Publisher Services